THE TRUTH ABOUT LOVE

Flor Ana

Cover Art Copyright © 2024 by Kayla Bauman
Illustrations Copyright © 2024 by Naomi Nguyen

Edited by Athena Edwards

1st Edition | 01
Hardcover ISBN: 979-8-9890939-2-2

Also Available in Paperback
ISBN: 979-8-9890939-9-1

First Published February 2024

For inquiries and bulk orders, please email:
indieearthbooks@gmail.com

Printed in the United States of America   1 2 3 4 5 6 7 8 9

Indie Earth Publishing Inc.
| Miami, FL |

www.indieearthbooks.com

INDIE EARTH
PUBLISHING

PRAISE FOR THE TRUTH ABOUT LOVE

"The sweetest concoction, a delectable tea cake of dreamy metaphors and confectioned rhyme. Flor Ana serves poetic spoonfuls of melodic medicine to mend the heart at any stage, kneading together innermost hurts, deepest desires, and the pillowy meringue of love in its purest form. *The Truth About Love* nourishes, satisfies, and leaves one wanting more—all at once; a baked-up treat to feed every deep feeling heart in the world."

—ELIZABETH KNIGHTLY, Author of *Choose To Choose Me*

"Once again, Flor Ana mesmerizes with gorgeous imagery, touching illustrations, and thought-provoking references. From a sweaty New York night to a chilly one under Christmas lights, her work teleports you to different places and phases of relationships. You're left remembering all the gooey sides of love, and most importantly, that it's worth it."

—MARLINA MOSSBERG, Author of *Peach*

"Soul touching, aching, reverberating, longingful, descriptive, exhilarating, juicy, beautiful, and sweet. Flor Ana writes in one of the most beautiful ways I have ever seen. I can't imagine a better way to spend my time than reading *The Truth About Love*."

—AMELIE HONEYSUCKLE, Author of *What Once Was An Inside Out Rainbow*

"*The Truth About Love* is equal parts love letter to, and poetic biography of, love itself. Flor Ana's powerful verses cast their warm glow on this driving force of humanity and illuminate the different shapes love can take when it walks through your door. This beautiful collection is sure to bring out the vulnerable romantic in all of us. "

—AZURE HALL, Author of *Reflections: A Mythology of Poetry & Prose*

"*The Truth About Love* pulls at your heartstrings in every which way. This book is delectable."

—KENDALL HOPE, Author of *The Willow Weepings*

"A collection filled with the fanciful nature imagery that's her trademark metamorphosed, Flor Ana applies the rawness that accompanies heartbreak, triumph, and affection in the day-to-day world. Flor straps us on her back as she navigates how the idea of love becomes the reality of love over time, a journey worth taking, as she holds a mirror to the reader; challenging us to define the undefinable because the magic lies in the attempt. "
—RENZO DEL CASTILLO, Award-Winning Author of *Still*

"If you're looking to manifest love and romance into your life, *The Truth About Love* unlocks your heart and sets you in the vibration to attract it. It's the ultimate Valentine's poetry book that's easy to read. And if you have given up on love, this book just might make you a believer again. "
—ANNIE VAZQUEZ, Author of *My Little Prayer Book*

"*The Truth About Love* is the truth, the whole truth, and nothing but the truth on the persistent enigma that unites the human race in its confusion and beauty—love. With succulent, ethereal visions, Flor Ana ruminates on the many facets of love—both the difficult heartbreak and the dreamlike romance—by deftly weaving wry wit and passionate yearning. The myriad environments and scenarios Flor takes the reader through will leave you with a luscious syrupy sweet taste in your soul. "
—PAUL LUNAIRE, Author of *On The Edge Of Burnout*

"*The Truth About Love* takes each of your senses on a dance. You will feel the shimmer of stardust, see the shine of sun and love, taste the fermentation of fruit and pleasure. Read this to affirm what you already know and feel or to remember what you may have forgotten; love is all there is."
—CHARLES MCCASKILL, Author of *Where I've Laid My Head*

"Flor Ana divulges an ancient secret that many of us have forgotten: love lives within. This collection of poetry is smooth and sweet, like honey and butter on a salted biscuit. Flor's words create a beautiful dance upon canvas that truly immerses you into the moment."
—JOHN QUEOR, Author of *Bypass*

THE TRUTH ABOUT LOVE

Flor Ana

Illustrated by Naomi Nguyen

LOVE CONTENTS

LOVE CONTENTS

LOVE CONTENTS

For Melodic Medicine,
scan here

Author's Note:

Dear Reader,
This collection you are about to embark on is love itself. It is a testament to love over time and the synchronicities and serendipities it holds, no matter who is holding them, no matter when. *The Truth About Love* began as a thought almost six years ago, to be titled '*A Love Beyond The Cosmos.*' You'll see hints of that initial spark still in the myodesopsias and margins of this collection through the recurring element of the cosmos and love as a cosmic force. What you hold here is my heart, and everything I've held close for so long, until it felt ready to be released into the ether, into your hands, into your heart. What you hold are poems that have been sitting patiently, sweetly, in a notebook for you to read, poems that have been years in the making, and poems that have emerged from my heart recently as it has continued to grow and age with every experience, every adventure, every heartbeat. Here you'll find that love is a plethora of things; you'll find that it is messy, it is kind, it is honest, it is abundant, it is... everything. And the truth is, you probably already know this, even if you haven't yet admitted it to yourself. I hope you find pieces of yourself in the love you are about to experience through my eyes. I hope you find the love I have for you, Reader, in between the lines of this collection, for your support is infinitely meaningful to me. And if you take anything from my words, please let it be this: *Love,* dear Reader, *always, simply, whole-heartedly, love. Even if it feels difficult, or vulnerable, or intimidating. Love can be the answer you've been waiting for.*

- *Flor Ana*

i bite the fruit of our nectar
and the cosmos swirl before me
in secretions of sugar
like simple syrup

love is a plump, ripe plum
a nectarine, a passionate peach
stripped to the pit by the loving tongues
of ethereal connection

love is the universe,
the galactic spiral of ebb and flow
that lives in the fruit bowl
for all hands to sip and savor

the cosmos drip off my lips
and i kiss the stars,
counting the confessions of love
written in the comets

the seeds i lick are
the ones that have been picked
by the gods beyond our knowledge and they show us love
through the sweetness and sour we crave to devour

5

Love is messy

7

For the broken hearts that have healed;
for the broken hearts in need of healing

PEITHO'S SONNET

many mighty men may come for me
but none will win my heart
nor will they dismantle my dignity
for persuasion is my art
ball of twine and cooing dove i hold
i am the herald of aphrodite
not many stories of me are told
but i promise you i'm rather almighty
mount olympus, how i love its gardens in summer
find me in the rose blossoms dining on a golden pear
guiding a knightly and handsome newcomer
seducing him sweetly and softly with my charming stare
now, i wasn't always like this, and i have known love's token
but no longer am i that kindred spirit, for he left my heart broken

KNOCKING AT HEARTS

knock knock knock

i'm tired of knocking
on the doors to your heart

it feels like no one's home,
but i could've sworn
i saw a light on,
a hand moving away from the window

matter of fact,
i have a text
and it states
come on over,
love me because i love you

but now i'm here
and i'm knocking
and i'm knocking
and i'm knocking,
waiting for you to open the door
because i don't want to knock on any other one

knock knock knock

hello?
anyone home?
i have a hole
the size of this doorframe
in my chest
and i refuse to leave my heart in a mailbox

i'm here
please tell me, dear,
do i leave?
should i stay?
should i go?
i am not soliciting my love to the neighbors, no
i've wrapped it up nicely, neatly, in a sparkly blue bow
and it's meant simply, only, wholeheartedly
for you

       knock knock knock

let me in,
or put up the foreclosure sign
that states your heart is no longer here

TRUST IS A TRICKY THING

trust is a tricky, fickle thing,
        easily tarnished
                like cheap gold ruined by sweat
trust can be tossed aside,
        like the leftovers of yesterday we swore we'd devour
            but sometimes
                  meals only taste better when they've had a
                      moment to sit

trust is a thing that can get stronger with time,
        or rusts
            like the underbelly of a car that lives its days at the
                      beach

trust is a thing you can never see, but feel
        it is a swallowed nectarine (pit) in your stomach
            it is a thing that lingers,
                or is gone in a single breath—

                  a single heartbeat

HEART-HEAD-HEAVY

my heart and head are heathens,
competing to see who can be heavier

A BED FOR TWO SHOULD NOT HOLD THE OPINIONS OF THOSE WHO ARE NOT TANGLED IN THOSE SHEETS

empty threats by third parties
tarnish the sheets,
laying like liquid magma between
us on queen-sized mattresses on
linoleum floors

there's nothing to be done
because the past cannot be undone
so our choices are limited

"beds have been made and now
we must sleep in them,"
but i'm burning

the lava is beginning to bury
itself into my legs, my thighs;
i have a fever and the cold sweats can
only turn so much lava into obsidian

i know you're hurting too,
pain releasing like fumes
but our wounds are different
and i don't know if we can
get up

RUINED RUMINATION

to go to bed upset
is to not sleep at all
instead it's ruined rumination,
ears perked to the ringing of a call

HUMMING HORNETS

my heart is broken,
but it is my stomach that is in the pits
and there's a pulling in my gut
that sinks me down to the ground

if there is such a thing as
butterflies in bellies,
what i'm feeling instead is a
nest of hornets, humming hymns as they sting

DANTE'S INFERNO

your love, or lack thereof, is bringing forth
a sour sensation gnawing at my throat,
a burning like dante's *inferno*
that can't be tamed
no matter how much water i drink
i am engulfed, enflamed,
broiling
on the sidelines of your words,
waiting for their parallel actions to come hither

I HATE IT WHEN YOU DO THAT

how silly of me
to think
you'd listen,
if only for a second,
to my babbling mouth,
forgetting your ears
tune everything out

A DROWNED WHISPER IN THE AFTERMATH (LOST AND FEELING)

my mouth tastes like a hangover and dry throat
tequila still sits at the bottom of my stomach
singing last night's songs
matcha and ciabatta are called in to compensate
but it's no use

tears escape my tired eyes
as tears drip from my nose too
let sleep take me to the moon
where i'll use my phlegm-filled words
to say *i love you*

RAINDROPS ON CHEEKBONES

the sky sheds my tears
so that my eyes remain dry

DISTANCE

and god,
it felt so good
to feel your warmth against mine,
skin to skin.

but now,
my stomach is in knots.
you're gone, and it is
my heart who will miss you most.

HOURGLASS HABITS OF THE HEART

habits are like hourglasses
and sometimes those grains
of sand grow sticky to the sides,
unable to come undone
sometimes you do unpleasant habits
only to find yourself
living in the ghosts of them,
and as the spectator, the outside source,
do you allow these habits to grow
back like weeds in the garden or
do you forever play the role of reminder?
a buzzing bee that says, "hey,
you're doing it again"
do you continue to be patient or
do you simply
give up
and pray to the gods that
those habits will dissipate
of their own accord?

OMISSIONS

i ask you
how your day has been
but really, what i want to say is
i miss you,
do you miss me too?

DO NOT DISTURB

i keep waiting
to hear from you
but every
notification
is a vibration
breaking my heart

A THREAD

i hold on to a thread,
      crimson like the heart that keeps me alive—
     although your silence has me dead inside

i hold on to a thread,
      with trembling scissors close enough to snip at hand—
       but my head is empty of commands

i hold on to a thread,
        and i can see that it is breaking
       but i don't know how to mend it—
       or should i just leave it aching?

i hold on to a thread,
        one i've never held before—

i hope my decision
is not one of later regret
        and i don't leave open
       a haunted door

DEAREST APHRODITE

Aphrodite, please hear my plea
bring a love that's true to me
let it be soft and let it be kind
let it extend past the fractures of time

Aphrodite, do you hear me calling?
i'm bit up and bruised from continuously falling
all that i ask is for a taste of what is sweet
i've been nothing but good; please, allow me this treat

Aphrodite, please, tell me you're there
i've got tears in my eyes and knots in my hair
broken bones and a voice that's almost gone
i've been writing you for weeks now, so please don't be long

Aphrodite, know i don't mean to sound desperate
but a sign—any sign from you—would be respite
a moment to breathe, to release all the ache
please, if you can hear me, don't allow me to break

...

Aphrodite, it's me, reaching out again
you said that'd you be here, but you didn't say when
i've been reaching out to you for a long eternity
taking slow, cautious steps to avoid uncertainty

Aphrodite, i'm begging you now
you're supposed to *be* love—i mean, that was your vow
you said giving up is not an option, but that's how i feel
at this point, quite frankly, i don't even know if you're real

...

Aphrodite, i no longer know what to say
you've been nothing but quiet, though i've written you every day
i've decided to keep going, but this time, without you
i guess you were right all along—*to love yourself is the only thing that's true*

THE DICHOTOMY OF LOVE

of the worst feelings,
nothing is quite like
a rejected hand,
dejected, grown
cold and calloused
from lack of warmth

love should be a thing
that lights,
that blooms,
that keeps both
hands and heart
emblazed in passion,
in love,
in heat

RUMORS

i've been ignoring it like the plague
talk that *love* fades
and slowly turns to dust

i want this feeling to last
is that too much to ask?
i don't want it to sit and rust

i want a *forever* kind of thing
don't care too much about the ring
instead, i just want to feel *wanted*

but if in the end it's true
and all 'love' is really doomed
then just know i'll forever be *haunted*

RIPE OR ROTTEN (THE EARTH WILL DEVOUR ME)

i desire to be desired,
to be wanted,
like fresh fruits oozing
their syrupy sweetness into the ground
instead of rotting into
summer skies dipped in sun,
forever longing

if no one picks me
from the bunch, off the tree,
sticks me in their pocket,
sinks their teeth into me,
at least the earth will savoringly
devour me

DRUNK OFF CACTUS WATER

i'm becoming accustomed to pain
and there's a faceless figure frowning
in my mind, biting its nails, begging
me to now allow myself to become
a numb, hollow ghost

on most days, the pain
wins and i water the gardens
of my blessings, my desires,
with the tears that pour
out of me,

but on the days where i'm
nothing but a desert,
heat waves feigning
a mirage of a smile scare me
because

what am i
if not
a houseplant that has learned
to express itself in the intricacies
of the cosmos?

HEART-SHAPED KNIFE WOUNDS

some of my
heart-shaped knife wounds
have been self-inflicted,
scars i turned a blind eye toward
but i guess it was never really *me*
instead, it was my mind,
thoughts that arrived
like great storm clouds

i've learned since then
that it wasn't that i annoyed you
with my love
instead, it was that i should've been
filling my own cup with sweet nectar
before i turned to fill yours

IRISES, THREE SIZES

i guess what i want is
for you to make me feel
like the only girl in your world,
the only girl for you;
to look into your eyes
and see love reflecting
off your irises as your
pupils grow three sizes

i guess i want to feel loved,
really loved;
a real love
that feels
soft, sweet, safe
one that feels
simple,
one that i'll never
question or doubt,
one that ends in
happily ever after
even if just for *now*

BECAUSE LOVE COULD NOT STOP FOR ME*

because love could not stop for me
i pleadingly stopped for it
the world reduced to simply feeling
and the hope for finding

i looked for it meticulously under every flowerbed
and every time i thought i found it,
i found something else
instead

i searched for it everywhere,
always just out of grasp
in the sparks of a kiss
in the eyes of a man

but i shouldn't have – it would've found *me*
no, i shouldn't have stopped for love at all
for love that's chased isn't *love*
and always leaves

because love could not stop for me
i reduced it to a fairytale
and that left me in agony,
for all i'd done was bound to fail

since then – 'tis centuries – but finally
i've learned what love can be
and while i was trying to stop for love,
i had not realized love had already stopped for me

**An ode to Emily Dickinson*

FULL-FLEDGED AND FLESHY

my heart feels heavy with longing
longing to be held, be touched
touched by hands that heal
heal the hurt that can be seen
seen through unknown eyes in theory
theory is the only thing that is
stopping the longing from becoming
a full-fledged, fleshy thing within my chest
because... what if it's only that you
don't love me in my head?

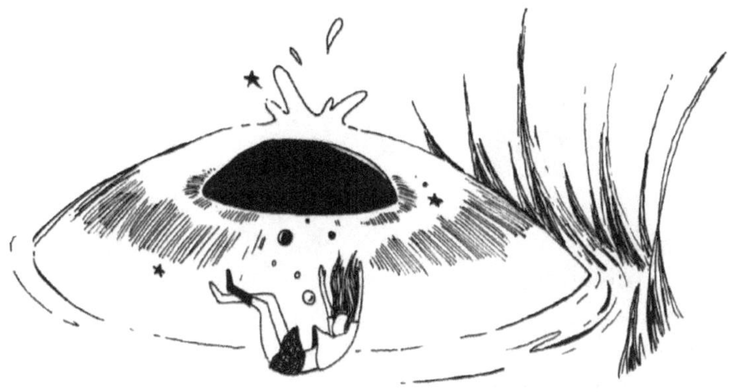

SYRUP

there's a syrupy linger
at the back of my throat
every time i swallow

it's a sweet aftertaste
for my salted afterthoughts
and i find myself craving
our pancake afternoons,
but it has always been just me
who eats them

molasses melt into me
like i wish i could melt
into you

and i pray that this
lingering saliva syrup
will be drowned by
the sweetness of your kiss
and not the salt of your saltines

LOVE IS A CHOICE

and my heart aches
at the tears and the breaks
in us by our own hands
and *god,* how i love you,
how i never knew one could love
this
much
and i want us to bounce back
from our bumps and our scrapes and our bruises

because, baby,
where there are scars left behind,
i promise you i'll kiss them,
lick wounds
until we're both healed and our hearts
are fully mended

through thick and thin,
i will continue to choose you
through the good and the bad
i know you'll stay too

BE CAUTIOUS OF WHAT YOU WISH FOR (IT MAY BE BETTER THAN YOU THINK)

i want to be loved, i deserve to be loved
i AM loved,
but why do i fear losing it?
why do i fear what it is, *really*?
because it is not how the movies show it
it is not the stories i read, the pages i linger on

i wish so heavily to be freed of this chase
and accept that i have FOUND love,
and that it is a *real* love,
a fleshy thing that holds my heart,
nestles it against its own and nourishes and nurtures

in ways, it is not what i thought it would be,
but in ways,
it is *oh so much* better
than anything i could have ever imagined

CLAIR DE LUNE PLAYS WHILE THE MOON GIVES ME CLARITY

the moon keeps me
company as i wait for you

the moon reminds me
of my greatness,
the one achieved, to be achieved,
with or without you

the moon and i sit
hand in hand, merry in our own company

because of the moon,
i no longer wait for you
instead, i am waiting
for the greatest version of myself

43

Love is kind

45

For the lovers and the loved

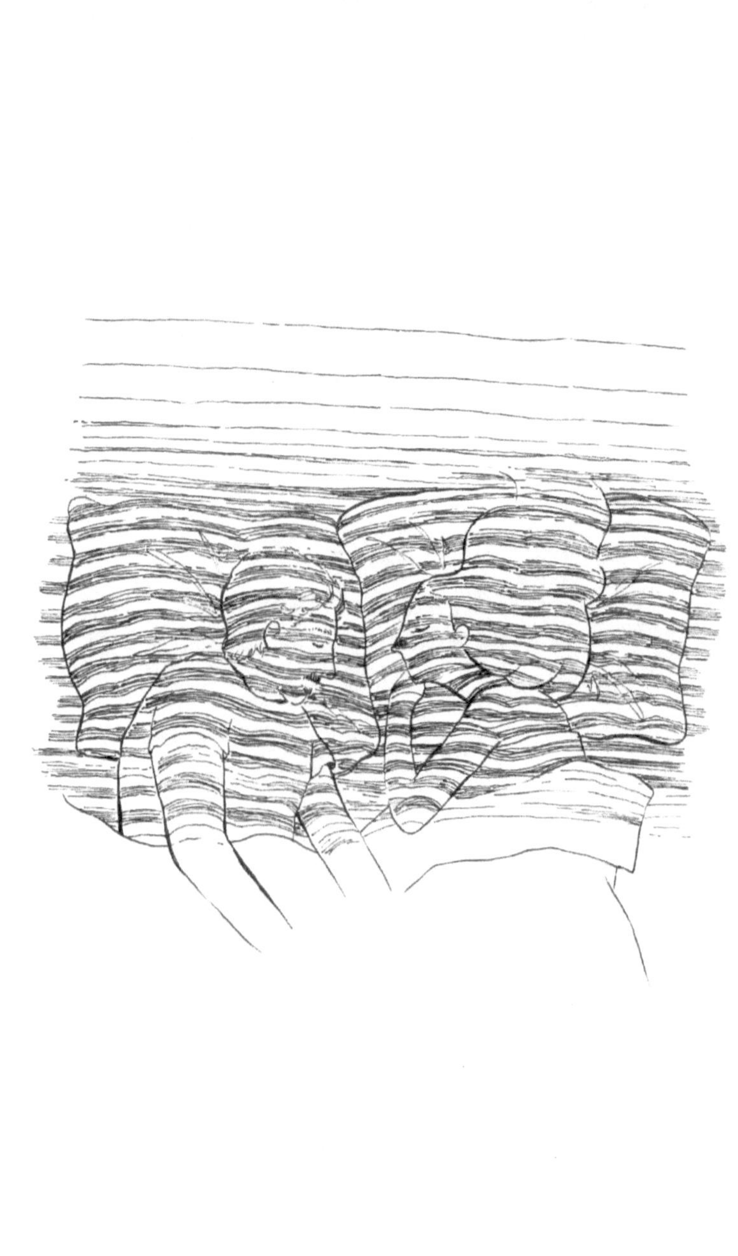

TISSUEY TAMINGS

rose petals tickle
the tinctures of a time
spent daydreaming in lullabies
and my irises grow three times
at the sun-warmth laughter
of your love

lips caressed thumbs
as doves
come hither from the nowhere
they've been cuddled in
and occupying

the sunlight is the light shining in
your eyes and your eyes are
the crown-jeweled cosmos
that expand and explode
in makings ethereal

rose petals bloom and burrow
in the soft tissuey tamings
of my heart
and every cavity fills with the
sweetness of adoration

A LOVE LETTER

i'm blessed to have met you,
blessed to have caught your eye
and you caught mine
and i remember it so vividly

you,
radiating
this beautiful, positive energy
never had i wanted more
to know a soul
behind chocolate eyes

blame it on the music,
the way you danced
or your vibrant smile
but
every day,
i fall harder
and more in love
with you

you have brought back
color
to a world that was
fading into black, white and gray

our love is unbreakable,
unstoppable,
the universe itself

we are not perfect
(*no being is*),
but at least
it seems
we are *perfect* for each other

you are
the soil in the ground,
the clouds in the sky,
the stars of the night
and i
am the flowers to your soil,
the wind moving your clouds,
the planets accompanying your stars

together,
we enchant
the world,
with our love,
brightening
even the darkest of nights

SYMPTOMS OF LOVE

with each inhalation,
another caterpillar comes out of its chrysalis,
a butterfly in my stomach

my heart begins to race
at the thought of your touch,
your kiss on my neck,
your lips on my lips

sweet sweat slicks my hands
as i inch closer to hold yours
and when
our fingertips touch,
mingling with each other in sparks,
more butterflies awaken

SIRIUS MAY BE THE BRIGHTEST STAR IN THE NIGHT SKY

sirius may be the brightest star in the night sky,
but you shine brighter
with every confident step
you take on this earth,
encouraging others
to follow their dreams
and do so
seriously

your smile
lights up
the room
like would the sun
when the clouds
finish traveling
through windy routes,
warming themselves
as they bask in your rays

sirius may be the brightest star in the night sky,
but your eyes
are galactic,
two brown puddles of cosmos
with black holes at their centers,
making love and life
instead of *taking* love and life away

LOVE LETTERS ARE OVERRATED

love letters are overrated,
but i'd love to see
the way you
curve your Y's
when you write
'i love you'

love letters are overrated,
but to see your handwriting,
each pen stroke,
neat and tight
or messy and bubbled,
would make me love you more

love letters are overrated,
but to receive one from you
would be a cosmic miracle;
an artifact to age gracefully
in the museum of my heart

STABLE, SWEET, SOFT

we don't need to talk
because just lying here,
caressing the pages of a story,
you next to me,
playing your guitar so sweetly,
energies bouncing off one another,
showcases our love

it's making music together
with words unsaid—
just strings and melodies that
fill the air with all that is,
and that is
and always will be
love

HOT SUMMER NIGHTS (MID-JULY)

i miss the hot summer nights
i have yet to experience
the ones where my skin is silky
with sweat
and the hum of a fan
reminds me of ocean waves
where i wear nothing but
an oversized t-shirt
—and it's not like
i wear bras anyway—
we're in new york city,
squished into four walls,
one meek window
and puddles form in armpits
and pearls form over lips
and despite the heat,
on the tip of my tongue
is the lust for the touch
of your lips,
for your arms wrapped
around my hips,

but the heat is unbearable
and we can barely be in
close proximity
until the silence of night settles,
bringing with it
an air of speakeasy,
and suddenly,
—although i've been dreaming about it
over our fever dreams and hot sweats—
you're irresistible
and i make my way onto your lap,

and despite the heat,
we can't seem to pull away
and we kiss,
and we kiss,
and we kiss,
making a hot summer night
of our own accord

FAITH

you can have too little
but never too much
and in the night,
when i crave your touch,
i remember that you're here with me
though miles apart,
and like a symphony,
the thought of you warms me up
because with you,
i have found the cosmos and
no black hole can swallow our love
because we are the universe itself
experiencing love through being
and thank you for being
here with me
always, like the air i breathe
though miles apart
and it is because of one thing:
faith

BESAME MUCHO

butterflies roam my belly
as if i were a sea, a meadow
of wildflowers

your fingertips touch my cheek
and i turn to cherry vanilla ice cream
left to melt in the sun for hours

i know where this is going—

i lick my lips
and you lick yours,
our breaths share a secret

it leaves a tingling
in my chest
that makes my tongue sweat

closer, baby, closer—

our mouths are all over each other—

we've become two little kids
full of glee, laughing nervously,
falling in love with one another

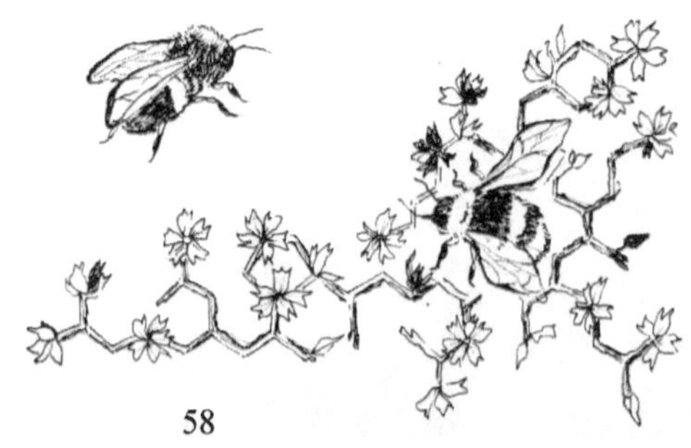

STARDUST AND SWEAT

we are a tangle of limbs,
chocolate-covered pretzels
melting into the backseat
of my very berry BMW
and oh,
the windows are so fogged,
so condensed that
the air is sticky,
thick like sweet condensed milk
and we melt into each other

we are navigating
the stars;
intergalactic, you and me,
sweat like sheen over our warm bodies,
and when we reach our destination,
hot kisses and blood pumping and hearts pounding,
we'll explode
like colliding stars,
our stardust the makings of magic

BEYOND THE COSMOS

our love is a love beyond the cosmos,
beyond the gray clouds that
bring summer rain, and the tastes of
sweet ice cream on hot tongues, caressed

our love is both the journey and the destination,
where we take turns behind the wheel,
sharing snacks and stopping
for baby brown bear cubs

our love is the licks of your guitar,
the strokes of my pen on notebook paper,
and we meet in the middle to see
what comes of this sweet-bliss encounter

and we fall in love
every kiss,
every breath,
every smile,
every time

MARSHMALLOW

sticky sugar sticks to my teeth
teeth that chatter unintentionally
unintentionally craving your gooey sweet
sweet like the kisses once given to me

me and you aren't stuck like glue
glue isn't sticky enough, strong enough; instead, we're marshmallows
marshmallows growing gooier by the fire
fire fueling us both with sweet desires
desires that cause my body to ache
ache like my teeth after eating too much sugar

sugar drips from my lips, from my hands and feet
feet that walk to you, no matter what streets
streets may separate us but i'm sure to once more find you
you are my love and together, baby, we're sweet fondue

NECTARINE VOICEMAILS

i want to be that nectarine,
the one that's rosy and ripe and
ready for teeth
sink them into me
let my syrupy sweetness drip
off the corners of your lips
let me lick
that sticky residue
let me be your morning sun,
let me be your sunset sky
i want to be the one that
makes you believe that pigs can fly
i want to be
the most desirable woman you've ever
laid eyes on
that way when you're holding me close,
in the cool, starry hours of twilight,
you'll realize all the blessings
you never want gone
sink your teeth into me
let me wear your smile
dance with me in the rain
write me a love letter
let's get away for a while
the universe had destined
for us to find each other, so
let's make this last
let's make the cosmos blush
let's be all we need,
slow and steady and in a rush

TULIPS

tell me how sweet
a treat it would be
if our two lips
met like tulips,
dancing together
amidst a wild garden
in the spring

i lick and bite mine,
feeling divine
at the thought
of your lips grazing—
they're dazing,
and i cannot get enough

tell me how sweet
a treat it would be
if our two lips
met like tulips
amidst a heavenly garden,
and darlin'
i know you see it too

like the light of the moon,
my evenings and days are never lonesome
because of you

ROMANCING THE WORDS (ABECEDARIAN)

romance speaks its own language:
alleviating the ache
blissfully & beautifully baked
coded in cuddles & kisses
dreamy & dearth of disses
ethereally elevated
fruitfully fated
gummy & gooey & gardenly gated
heart-full, never only half the time
it speaks isms & for that i'm
jaded, jeweled by the gestures of joy
kissed by the lips of kindness kinned coy
lovingly, romance laughs in my locket
merry & marvelous, i keep it in my pocket
never forgetting its near my heart
oath of oasis, oozing of art
precious romance, passionate & pure
quaint & quintessential, quixotic you cure
ravenous for you, romance, i'm rhapsodic
serendipitous & saccharine, please don't be spasmodic
together, we can tame with tenderness
unconditional, you are utterly, undyingly measureless
venerating vulnerability, you're my forever valentine
warmhearted & whimsical, with you i'll never whine
xoxo, romance, you are my xanadu
yearn for you, yowl of love, i do
zestfully, you are the zenith, the zing i choose

DESERT DEVOTIONS

i hand you my heart
for it is deeply devoted
to every fiber of your being

i devour every moment
spent with you
leaving bits of it between my teeth to savor later

if my heart were an oasis
you would be every particle of water
i want to swallow

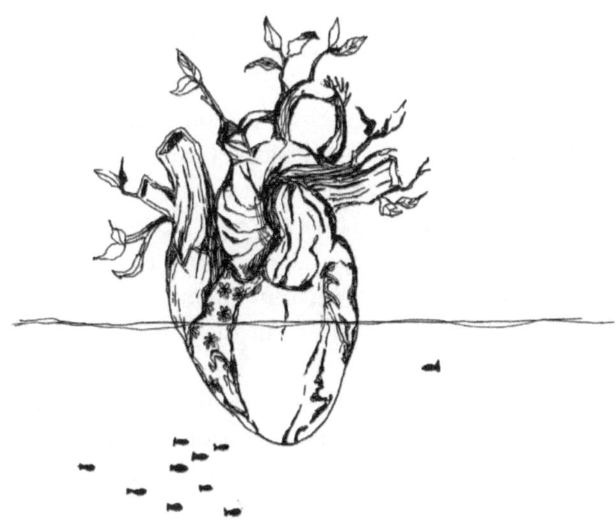

ALTERNATE TIMELINES

January 14, 1963: a day I'll never forget. We've just hiked 4.2 miles, sweat on our brows, twig scratches on our arms from going off the trail and exploring something untouched. Somehow, at 12,000 feet elevation, we stumble upon an unexpected waterfall. With the heat shining brightly above, it doesn't take long before we undress and run into the frigid, yet tranquil waters. Too cold to stay for long, we refresh ourselves, laying down on the warm rocks, letting the sun dry us with its powerful rays. I was looking at the waterfall when you asked me a question that took me for a turn.

"Have you ever been in love?"

Suddenly, I feel as if I am back in the water. Numb. Frigid. Naked. How could you ask such a question? You know I've loved you since the moment I met you. I look at you. Despite knowing each other for eight years, having lived together, been together, been apart and having found ourselves back here again, the look in your eyes is different. While I am normally the one to lay my vulnerability on the table, now, it feels you are.

I clear my throat. "You know the answer to that question. Why do you ask?"

You run a hand through your wet hair and look down at the water, avoiding my stare. I feel my insides turning inside out wondering what is running through your mind.

Without looking at me, you turn and say, "I never thought I'd know love. Real love. But the way you look at me, the way you continue to love me despite all the tribulations, tempers and tears, the way you're still here... it all just shows me that I've been loved this whole time."

You turn to me, and there's a softness there, in the way your brows rest above your eyes, in the way your lips open and close as if looking for more words to say. I stay quiet, knowing I'm exposed, knowing you see me. See all I'd do for you. Now, it is me who's turning away, avoiding the gaze you're greeting me with. I am naked above a pedestal I did not know I had signed up to be on.

You clear your throat, willing the words you need to say, the words I know in the deepest cavities of my heart.

"I've been in love. With you. It's always been with you. With every version of you. And I know I don't say it much. I know I sometimes don't show you love in the language of your own tongue, but I do love you. I have always loved you. Even when it has been me that didn't want to see it. But I see it now. Just as I see God in the way the sun glimmers above the water. Just as I see you. All of you. I love you, and from this point forward, I want to make sure that's never lost, to myself nor to you."

LOVE STORY MEMOIRS

i fill with eunoia
at the thought of you
with those big brown eyes
and that laugh you do
i can't help but fall in love with you
and that, *my love*, is the honest truth

you are more than my sun,
my moon and my stars;
you are my whole galaxy
and this universe, it's *ours*
in our irises live our love story memoirs
and we drink the sweet nectar of a love's reservoir

let us whisper sweet *everythings*
as we lay tangled in the night
and that smile of yours, *my god*, how it shines so bright
come away with me; be the muse i always write
where love and light always know to win the fight

KISMET

we lock eyes
lips tingling for touch
our hands meet

                          no amount of distance
                          can keep us apart,
                          can keep us from
                          returning

                  to

          other
each

we lock eyes,
and i can't help but feel
this is   *kismet*

i have found my star
in a universe of millions,
i have found my star,
despite all the trials and tribulations

                        meant to keep us apart
                        meant to make us

                stronger

my darling, we lock eyes
and i easily see your soul

          how beautiful it is to be by your side
          how beautiful it is to have found each other

AMOROUS CONGRESS

interlocked hands that bring warmth + love
kisses all over, pure as a dove
the connection of two souls
two heartbeats transcending into one

the heat kicks in + tickles your skin
your body relaxes and you let it all in
every stroke, every kiss, sharing love from within
an act of love, unity, nature + connection

THE EARLY BIRD FELL IN LOVE WITH THE NIGHT OWL AND THE EVENING OWL FELL IN LOVE WITH THE MORNING BIRD

i am morning and you are night, but
we like
to meet in the middle, in
the afternoons and
laugh like young lovers,
talk like old ones,
kisses cosmic

i am dawn and you are dusk, but
when we meet at noon,
we are both night and day
light and dark
the complete kismet equation of
true love

i am sun and you are moon, but
trust me when i say
the universe knows this to be true
love,
so we'll continue
meeting in the middle,
and when others look up
into the sky
and see you and i—
the sun and the moon sharing the blue—
they'll know just how much
we're unwilling to just work our light shifts,
unable to stay away from each other

HUMAN COMFORT IN DECEMBER

and we found sleep
in the warmth of an embrace,
folded knees and breathing bellies
acting as blankets,
your breath on my shoulder as soothing
as crashing waves at midnight

we were a mess of stretched limbs,
two bodies caressed into one
while snow fell in northern nights
and crickets chirped to
Christmas lights

PROFESSING A PAINTED PORTRAIT OF DESIRE

i want to capture the profession of your love
in words
so i can transpose it to a notebook and
read it blushingly behind closed doors
but i'm done asking you to write me
a love letter
so i'll settle for a love text
sealed with a kiss
a message a paragraph in length
showing your most vulnerable insides

open up, honey
my arms are open and awaiting you warmly
i promise to never let you fall
so long as you look at me with those
big brown eyes like you did
that first time we kissed, when
the world shifted in your red truck
and i tasted love for the first time
my lips were bruised with your being
and i wanted it all again

i'll profess my love for you in words
like ocean waves sing hymns to the moon
serenading it with a gust and a hush
and if this is all too cheesy for you
then grate me instead
sprinkle me on your favorite dish
and devour my delicacies

MEASUREMENTS

your neck
is the perfect length
for me to nuzzle my head
and rest on your shoulder

your hands
are just the right size
for interlocking fingers that
feel safe

your height
is just right
for the forehead kisses
you bless me with that i so often crave

your smile
is my warming sun,
melting the frost off my fingertips
on the coolest of days

your eyes
are sweeter than the chocolate they resemble
and i can swim in them
for eternity to come

your soul
was made for loving mine
and mine was made
for you, my love

CONFESSIONS WHISPERED BY COSMOS

and so i have a confession
and that is that i love you,
like end-of-world-
and-i'm-screaming-your-name-into-the-cosmos
love you,
and i'm scared
scared that you could never love me
as much as i love you
or that, over time, my love
will be in vain
because life changes and people grow old and bold and—
what if we grow apart?
what if the cosmos only destined our paths
to cross momentarily?
i'm scared of the *what ifs,*
of the feeling in my chest that's heavy when
i think of a life without you,
of tears forming in my eyes at the
thought of my heart heaving
broken into a million pieces

and i can write this all down and
think if or if *not* to tell you
but the truth is
a part of me wants to shed my clothes and
show you my nakedness, my rawness
the parts of me that are
vulnerable
a part of me wants to share this with you
in the hopes that you will tell me
exactly how you feel so i can

pin it to my heart, cherish it forever
and have the faith i need to know that we
are indeed written into the cosmos, that
our love will go beyond the mountains of the gods
and we will hold each other and hold each other and hold each other
warm and soft, for all lifetimes to come

HEAVEN-SENT

meeting you was heaven-sent,
loving you was god's way of showing me
that there is indeed
such thing
as true love,
as love beyond time and space,
as love that continues to find itself
in other worlds, in other lifetimes

i found heaven in your arms
and now i hear
the angels sing soft hymns
every time the words
'i love you'
escape your lips like
the sweetest melody
i have ever heard

honey,
you are my muse,
you are the reason
my heart hums
sweet symphonies
that i can't help but
transpose to paper

COINCIDENTAL CONNECTION

there's a chance
had our parents not left
the motherland
we could've met
on the prettiest island
there's ever been

perhaps it would've been
in a *seiva* classroom
or picking berries in the fields,
in *el circulo social*
or in a march
to overthrow the government
where we would
run off
hand in hand
before they could catch us
and throw us in cells

we'd escape to *Varadero*
or climb to the peak of *Pico Turquino*,
eventually escaping the motherland
altogether
through air or sea
all for a chance at a life full of blessings and liberty

we wouldn't forget our struggles,
we'd let them keep us grateful
we'd think of all we once lived through
and cry tears of joy for having been able to
safely get away

had our parents not escaped
the motherland
perhaps we could've melt
in the place of *lindos paisajes*
and then left to *el pais de los sueños*

perhaps we'd end up
exactly where we are
today: *juntos*

LOVE CAN MAKE DREAMS COME TRUE

"and who knows, baby? maybe this book of love will be the one that does it, that helps me to achieve this dream and *make it*—whatever that really means—as a writer, as the author i want to be. and maybe, baby, i'll have enough money for a place to call my own and you can join me there if you'd like and together we can make it a home and finally be able to say good night instead of goodbye when the crickets begin to chirp and the moon's shine is a glittering eye in the sky. think about it. imagine it. we could host dinner parties, walk around naked like adam and eve once did, and make love and laugh and dance and learn to fall in love all over again..."

i'm sure there's a sparkle in my eye, because i look at you and you're smiling, eyes crinkling so much that i wish i could memorize those creases for eternity to come. i smile back, kissing your soft knuckles and you lovingly reciprocate the act.

"this book could be my dream come true," i add. "this book could be it."

and there's that smile again. the love in your eyes. the support. the belief in my dreams, in me, and suddenly, out of my peripherals, i see my own reflection. the love in my own eyes. the twinkle for the future, wanted, already written and on the way.

love, i say to myself, like a soft whisper, a breeze dancing on the petals of a velvet flower, *love is the answer. love can be what makes dreams come true.*

I WILL FOREVER FIND YOU

our souls, my love,
have collided in such a way
that i know that we go
beyond this lifetime

our love, my love, is the universe itself,
an exploration that goes deep, deeper,
hinting at shared cells that will
continue to find each other,
fight for each other,
choose each other,
past infinity and whatever cosmic explosion
eventually causes us to drift apart,
awaiting our reunion once more

two halves don't make a whole, baby,
we both know that,
but two wholes have come together
to create something beautiful,
something that brings tears of joy
to the eyes of god and inspires the
melodies of the angels

i have found the whole i belong with,
the one that pushes me to become the sun,
the one that loves me indefinitely and unconditionally,
mirroring the love that grows within me

my whole heart calls out your name,
and no matter what,
what lives are lived beyond this one,
beyond this realm, beyond this experience,
i will forever find you, my love

Love is everything

87

For everyone and everything
(if you look closely, you'll find reason to live, and that is for love)

IT JUST DEPENDS ON HOW YOU LOOK AT IT

for some,
love fades,
becoming a task,
a part of the routine,
losing its magic
with every new day,
becoming mundane

for others,
love is everywhere:
in the flowers,
in the stars,
in the soft breaths of the skies
essentially,
in everything

ALL TOO WELL

when we are alone
we are
our truest selves

or perhaps with the loved ones
the ones
that know us *all too well*

A VICTORIAN SELF-LOVE AFFAIR

and she said *wait*,
though she did not say what for,
and the realization came late
as rose petals fell on sleek floors
her whole world turned red,
a shade of crimson never seen before,
and she took her heart to bed
in a loving last forevermore

she learned to love herself
in the glory of imperfection
wisdom came from prose on shelves
as she longed for pure connection
in the mirror, she learned love,
that in her smile lives affection
and that her soul is pure as dove,
ready to cherish her self-reflection

LOVING IN HAIKU

oh, love knows no hate
instead, it listens sweetly
like stars to wishes

AS YOU WISH

i deserve to be cherished,
to be serenaded
with a beatbox outside my window
or music blasting from outside the door with
a song picked especially for me
i deserve to be the woman of your dreams,
the woman you wish to hold in your arms
even when i'm crying a river,
even when i'm not feeling myself
i deserve to be gifted bouquets of flowers
and kissed from head to toe,
adored in private and in public
i deserve it because i work at all i do
i deserve it because i do nothing but love you
i deserve it because i don't meet you halfway but
show up on your doorstep with your
favorite takeout and a kiss on the lips
i deserve to be loved like they do in movies,
in books, in fantasies that seem so far from
this world because i am out of this world
i am celestial, divine, a goddess in disguise
and i deserve to be worshiped, just as i
worship you

FALLING (A LOVE POEM)

falling out of love is a volcano awaiting eruption,
lying in bed alone and choking on olives,
a cat that knows nothing but scratching and scratching and scratching,
a letter of eviction from the heart you once thought could be home,
hours of confusion,
hours of *will it or won't it?*
hours of *will this even matter?*
falling out of love is a power outage,
a tsunami on the day you decide to go the beach,
rollerblades on your feet that leave blisters and make it hard not to sway,
it's missing smiles you thought would never go away,

but...

falling *in* love is sun rising
fiery passions and already pitted peaches,
a dog that knows tricks without being taught,
a love letter delivered in handwriting to the mailbox,
hours of love making
hours of laughing, talking, swaying,
hours of eating—homemade or takeout, it does not matter
falling *in* love is twinkling lights
the full moon over the shoreline
sticky, sandy toes entwined,
it's kisses that seem straight-sent from heaven

A WORD OF ADVICE

there's something soothing
about listening to the birds' song,
something wholesome about
loving with your whole heart
even when it tires you out
and pulls and stretches you apart
there's something beautiful
about being yourself,
something exciting about
opening your eyes to the magic
that lingers just beyond visible light
that you feel brush the tips of your fingers
reminding you of its presence

a word of advice:
if you're going to love,
always love yourself first,
and if you're looking for magic,
let the cosmos and the universe
quench your thirst

FLUCTUATIONS (LOVING IN WAVES)

sometimes,
love is a wave,
an ebb and flow
of emotion and passion,
of chaos and order,
of everything and nothing

sometimes,
love is a wave,
a spiritual symphony,
a crash and renew,
a come and go,
a love like no other

sometimes,
love is constant fluctuations,
a push and pull,
a tug at emotions
that are
beyond words,
beyond the explainable,
simply
felt

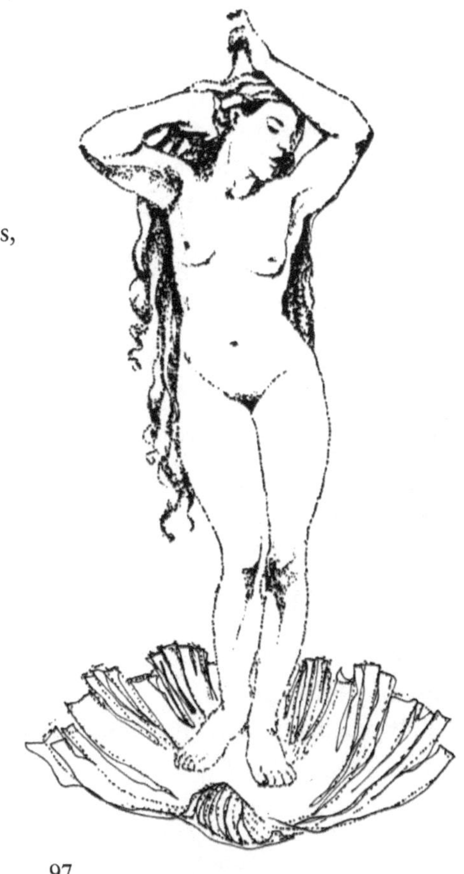

HABITUAL RITUALS

habitual rituals reside in my bones
and though i may get lonely,
i never feel alone

i've learned to trust my instincts
and the tinctures of sunlight on skin
like fruit flesh, sticky and ripe to the touch
it's truly a spiritual win

the sun no longer wakes me
instead, it's a morning sunless rewire,
and though i lay in bed
focused on breath and the butter roll thoughts
that roll down kitchen counters,
i continue to reach my desires

because habitual rituals may not always look the same
no, habitual rituals reside in a stay
of mind,
a dancing dime,
a maraschino memory,
it's a staircase that ascends
beyond the heavens
that you wear in the folds of your lobes like an accessory

and they linger
right there,
pulsing at your pineal gland,
traveling the distance of
bodily dreams and lavender-infused fantasy lands

habitual rituals readily prepare you
for the star-kissed, cosmic cuddles that are to come,
and even when loneliness strikes
like a match against the setting sun,
i know in the universe
there will always be love

WHAT IS LOVE? (A VIEWING OF LOVE LANGUAGES)

we all feel. whether we showcase it or not, and there are so many things to feel. some feelings have words to describe them and some do not, yet that does not make them any less valid. instead, it's... intriguing. how am i to describe this emotion, this feeling, this *thing* fueling my heaviest insides, if there does not exist a word for it? sometimes, there are multiple meanings, or interpretations, for what we feel—all of which can be interpreted differently by different people, different perspectives / and the truth is this: we all *love* differently. but sometimes we forget to see it that way, we forget to realize that we all share a unique combination of stars in our cells. we expect to be loved, but we expect it to be done in the way that *we* love— completely forgetting that this is not always the case, completely forgetting that, most times, it won't be. in your moments of despair, try to recall this little truth: everyone loves, but everyone loves differently, all valid in their own way / and just because you're not being spoken to in your love language does not mean you are not loved at all.

AND THE SUN SHINES AND SHINES

halos of angel-like light
fill a sky that is more
clouds than sun
it's a painting made by god,
all creations and artistic styles combining
to form one

somewhere in the world
someone is loving beyond
what they think is
their heart's extent
and i hope they are loved
in return,
loved with the same energy they're
putting in, because
love can be a beautiful thing—halos
of angel-like light that
fill the skies and i hope
the rains only come to bring
growth, and the sun shines and shines

WOULD LOVE SURVIVE APOCALYPSE?

God, let us pray it does—
because a world without love
is not a world worth living in

FAITH (II.)

faith is found in the birds' song
in the afternoon sun
in the streaks of clouds
and even in the shadows

faith is found in the dim candlelight
on stormy nights
and in the prayers you
tell yourself

faith can be found anywhere,
but mostly,
faith is found within
never let yourself forget it

AMOR SIN DECIRLO

lay me down in lavender grass,
i want to kiss the palms of our earth,
feel the embrace of our sun, brushing
against my blushing cheek
as i take deep breaths and *release,*

                  release,

                     release

APHRODITE'S RETURN (EKPHRASTIC ACROSTIC)*

Alas, love has been given a face of golden sun!
Pure and pretty, she sits in a
Hollow clamshell, clenching her heart.
Red runs through her, encrusted in passion,
Or is it empathy that drives her?
Desire to love and be loved
In return?
Time will tell, though she is forever
Encrypted in metaphor and prose,

> *a depiction of love*
> *made female,*
> *made gold.*
> *made god.*

**The Birth of Venus by Sandro Boticelli (1485-1486)*

KALEIDOSCOPE SUNDAYS

over sentient shores,
clouds part to reveal warm sun-kisses

they bruise my shoulders with love
and it's an oasis of a sunday

through the waves and waterways
love oozes, rises and crashes, and
the world itself becomes
a kaleidoscope

I'VE ALWAYS BEEN IN LOVE

i've always been in love,
with the tidal waves
that form in cotton candy skies,
their sugary sweetness,
a birthday-candle-blessing in disguise

i've always been in love,
with the clouds that cry in hidden spheres,
one teardrop for every lightpost passed
in the fields of wheat
and valleys of clementine grass

i've always been in love,
with the way persimmon petals prowl,
how they float in orderly fashion,
down the rivers of lilac velvet babylon
and i can taste the golden crowns
of a sun once swallowed whole

i've always been in love,
with the sounds of thunder, no match
for Beethoven's symphonies but
i am sure if we could ask him
he would call them siblings;
a snake eating itself

the sycamores and redwoods are
getting ready for bed
and the sun lazily lays down its belly
at the belly of the beast, but

luckily for me,
i've always been in love

FOUNDATION

let love be your foundation,
and you will never
drown in your sorrows

let love be your foundation,
and you will find reasons
to live beyond tomorrows

let love be your foundation,
and the reason for which
you give

let love be your foundation,
and you will be met
with all the life there is to live

let love be your foundation,
let it be
what picks you up when you fall

with love as your foundation,
you will have the ability
to do it all

THE TRUTH ABOUT LOVE

love is a verb,
often mistaken
for noun,
but
to love
is to take action,
to show your heart on your sleeve,
to love unconditionally,
to share your most vulnerable thoughts
with another,
without judgment

love is not *love*
without admiration
without affection
without patience
and forgiveness

love cannot *be love*
without action
without intent
without longing
and desire

the truth about love is that
it's simple,
simply complicated enough to
become messy,
to invade all your thoughts,
to be the sole reason your heart skips a beat,
beats uncontrollably
or stops beating entirely

everyone deserves to be *loved*,
to be truly *loved*,
to *feel* truly loved

because the truth about love is that
it is infinite,
infinitely majestic,
made of complex calculations of cosmos,
unable to be restrained to our man-made boxes

they could never hold enough s p a c e
for all that love *is*
and can be

SPRINGTIME IN AUGUST (EKPHRASTIC)*

Pierre-August Cot's *Springtime* has been haunting my computer tabs as i've wanted to write about it but come to a blank every time / and it's funny, in a way, that this painting i've seen—framed in houses, and once in its original form in an autumnal *New York*—has left me so speechless / but i guess that is a side effect of love; that it can be so strong that no amount of words said or even thought can compare, and perhaps, one day, i will come close—or perhaps i never will / *Springtime* is a locking of eyes, a warm caress, a swing that never stops serenading / it is comfort, a known that changes and you continue to know, to get to know, because you *choose* to. *Springtime* is a love beyond ages, beyond phases / it is a love that knows no end but simply metamorphoses with time, growing stronger, deeper / *Love* is a painting, one you never grow tired of admiring, and if you look closely, you'll see it is everlasting, ever encompassing everything / it is looking into the eyes of the cosmos themselves and finding your own reflection in the eyes of a lover, in the eyes of your mother, in the morsels that float in the universal dust

**Springtime by Pierre-August Cot (1873)*

THE SEED

love, my darling, is a unique thing,
it is here and it is not, it is felt but never seen,
it is waiting for you to be vulnerable, to feel its insides,
to open your heart

love, my darling, is a seed,
one you must choose to water daily,
one you choose to nourish and see grow
despite the heartful and heartless hardships

LOVE,

love is infinite laughter
it is falling down nine times
and getting up countless

love is happiness (in bulk)
it is a shoulder to cry on
at all times

love is a plethora of adventures
it is *falling* in love,
always and all over again

love is trust (above all else)
it is continuing to choose this love
every day

love is a lifetime of friendship
it the sunshine after every storm
(even if we have been the storm itself)

love,
in the end,
is absolutely everything

LOFI LOVE'S INCARNATE

rain pitters and patters at my window;
its sound and scent sit on the pedestal for
lazy afternoons and eyes dreamy and drunk off sleep

the sun parts and the clouds kiss the heavens;
light explodes in my line of sight and
air conditioning units roar as pens scribble words

i can hear it,
nature's heartbeat,
when i listen closely

i can hear the sounds of the ocean
like the buzzing of a bee,
hungry, thirsty and longing for the prettiest flower

and all of this brings out this desire
this longing, this want, this need
to be something remarkable, something extraordinary

i want to be the sun,
be love's incarnate, i want to be
the holy cosmos, a goddess galaxy

HYACINTHS, ROSES, DAISIES, SUNFLOWERS, ETC.

heal me wholly with hyacinths,
ready me for love with roses,
desire me daintily with daisies,
seduce me sweetly with sunflowers

i want to feel love felt through flowers,
through petals of pure delight,
of colors pure as earth and light
i want to feel the love of flowers,
and for the love of flowers,
i will,
for i am only a flower, too

ALLITERATE ME IN MAJESTY

my soul is made of strawberries;
sweet secretions slippery with song,
lavender lullabies of lyrical love,
chocolate pudding puddled by praying hands,
delectable deities dripping in dance,
honey homes of heavenly hymns,
berry-filled beauties buried to the brim,
honest intentions tickled by time,
merriment and mercury and nursery rhymes

my soul is made of orchids;
oasis of order and odor divine,
cosmic calendulas that calmly collide,
lilies of the valley sown softly into wedding veils,
dainty and delicate; never lacking in details,
nectar-like, natural, nourishing and neat,
harnessing the sun despite the summer heat,
ultraviolet and goddess-like, oh my,
born of love, laughter and heavenly sky

my soul is made of peonies;
plumped and primped for perennial bliss,
etched with an earthly ethereal kiss,
caught in the winds of wander and wonder,
thriving with timing and moving with thunder,
settling into sun, a light like the wild,
careful, yet carefree; complexities compiled,
glittering with gratitude, grins and grace,
fair and fawning for flowers embraced

A LOVE LETTER (TO SELF)

love, my precious, brave petunia. just love. fall in love with the colors of sunset, the sounds of the ocean waves, the verdant of lively trees, the rains that bring a cleansing and calm on tired nights, the thunder that gets your heart pumping and pounding in your light over the lightning strike-sparks that come with feeling love and being loved. fall in love with people, with everyone you meet; find the mirror of yourself in every soul you see. fall in love with the ways things change, with the pushes and the pulls, with the journey *and* the destination. just love, my precious, brave petunia. never forget to simply *love*.

SWEET DESSERT

love is like a piece of cake
feelings are the fillings
that fill with joy
sweet sugar of the heart
with every taste, every spoonful of memory

love is like *tres leches*
sweet, creamy, *dulce* and you just want to
soak in the ooey, gooey loving
letting the syrup drip
from parts no one else can see

love is like *flan*
tender, tended to
oozing with caramel and covered in coconut shavings
a nice decadent touch of crunch

love is like *tiramisu*
hook it up into an iv
jittery, jaded, jammed
with heart and it does nothing but
give and receive and give and receive (like a heartbeat)

love is simply sweet
a delicious delectable treat
a dessert one always wants to eat
that, with one bite, makes one feel complete

WE ARE LIKE LOVE SONGS

look closely,
listen sweet,
every being you encounter
is a loving soul to meet,
is a serenade
looking for muse,
is a love song
hoping to calm the blues,
is a being
just like us,
waiting for a light
at the edge of daily dusk

A CRY FOR LOVE

i see the good in people,
even the ones who don't deserve it
i see the good in people,
even the ones who make me feel deserted
i see the good in people,
even in the ones who do nothing but break me apart
i see the good in people,
and sometimes, it tears at my heart
i see the good in people,
and sometimes, i can't unsee it
i see the good in people,
so much so, i want badly to believe it
i see the good in people,
the bad erased and swept under the rug
i see the good in people,
especially when the going gets rough
i see the good in people,
even when my mind knows i shouldn't
i see the good in people,
because a life without love... i just couldn't

REMINDERS (ACROSTIC)

It is said that:

Love is everywhere. but sometimes, it feels
Over the rainbow, hidden somewhere where the
Verdant trees grow and
Everything is coated in rose gold.

You can get there, if you just believe,
Or maybe, you can't, and instead you must act and
Understand that tenacity is required to move forward, to

Show the world (and yourself) that things happen but
Only when you

Make things happen.
Unless you're lucky, you'll have to be the one to take chances, to make
Chances happen for you. to make love and light and dreams appear
                              before you, to cry those tears of
Happiness. It all takes effort and strength and time, but I know you
                              can do this. Just don't give up.

Love floats around us like cosmic dust.
    May every speck of silver and gold mean more love is to come.

ACKNOWLEDGMENTS

This collection would not have been possible without all the love that flows through my veins and lives in my little sphere of the universe; and i have so many loves to thank:

- *You know who you are,* thank you for your love and light. Thank you for showing me what love could be. Thank you for continously pushing me to strengthen my craft; to write, write, write and keep writing. I will always love you, infinitely.

- To my parents, *los adoro y muchas gracias por todo.* I wouldn't be here without you, in this country, in this life, in the letters of the words of these pages. Thank you for your love and support, and for always telling me that I had a voice. Yaima, Cairo, Lucia and Firas; *mis Mimas* and Bebe, thank you for your love and light, even when you haven't understood the world of poetry. *Los amo a todos.*

- To my goddess of an editor (with the perfect name), Athena, thank you for challenging me to better my poetry and my writing, and for all of your feedback. A book without an editor is not a book complete; thank you for helping me to complete this piece. It's always an honor to work with you.

- Liz, Kendall, Amelie, Johnny, Renz, Annie, Azure, Marlina, Alexandra, Paul, Charles, thank you for taking the time to read my words and provide your praise. This book now holds a little piece of your love for the same things I love—literature, poetry, art, and life.

- Naomi, as always, it is a pleasure working with you. I'm so glad we came together once more to create art out of poetry. Thank you a hundred times over for your beautiful illustrations.

- Kayla, thank you for your hard work in designing the anatomical heart that is the cover of this book. Thank you for your patience with me and for seeing this vision through with me. I know you put your heart into that heart; thank you so much.

- Indie Earth Publishing, you have been this blessing that I hadn't dreamed of having. It's been an honor to grow you and to grow *with* you. Thank you to all the authors I work with and to the beautiful, creative, inspiring, and supportive community we are creating.

ACKNOWLEDGMENTS

- To the art that inspires me; the words, the paintings, the songs, the tastes and smells, the nature, the Universe... *everything*. Thank you for allowing your light to reach mine.

- To *you*, dear Reader, thank you for your continuous support, whether this is the first time you've picked up one of my books, the third or the fifth. Because of you, I am following a dream and falling in love with the journey and adventure life is leading me on. Please, follow your dreams. They're possible so long as you work on them with love, and that is what I have for you: nothing but love.

OTHER WORKS BY FLOR ANA

Perspective (and other poems)

The Language of Fungi & Flowers

Nourish Your Temple: Self-Love & Care Poetry

A Moth Fell In Love With The Moon

OTHER WORKS FEATURING FLOR ANA

Stories From The Forest: 10 Stories of Nature, Love, Loss and Life

The Spell Jar: Poetry for the Modern Witch

Ardell Magazine Issue 02

Love Letters To The 305

Knight Rider Waves From Around The World

Glow: Self-Care Poetry For The Soul

The Spell Jar: Book of Shadows (Vol. II)

A Winter's Warmth: Short Stories To Keep Out The Cold

ABOUT THE AUTHOR

FLOR ANA is a Cuban-American writer, singer, and poet who loves to make people feel something through her words. She is the author of a handful of poetry collections, including *A Moth Fell In Love With The Moon*, which was a Finalist in Poetry for the 2023 American Writing Awards. Flor is also an event poet on occasion with her typewriter, and when she is not writing, she is helping other writers, being creative any way she can and indulging in time with her loved ones, food, travel and the universe and all its delicacies.

Connect with Flor on Social Media:

Instagram: @littleearthflower // TikTok: @floranawrites

www.floranawrites.com

About the Publisher

Indie Earth Publishing is an author-first, independent co-publishing company based in Miami, FL. A publisher for writers founded by a writer, Indie Earth offers the support and technical assistance of traditional publishing to writers without asking them to compromise their creative freedom. Each Indie Earth Author is a part of an inspired and creative community that only keeps growing.

www.indieearthbooks.com

Instagram: @indieearthbooks

For inquiries, please email:
indieearthbooks@gmail.com

www.ingramcontent.com/pod-product-compliance
Lightning Source LLC
Chambersburg PA
CBHW062213150726